Before You Step

Into Someone Else's Shoes

Before You Step Into Someone Else's Shoes

Sammy O. Joseph

PPH
Pulse Publishing House

Published in the United Kingdom by

Pulse Publishing House

Box 15129

Birmingham

England

B45 5DJ

pulsepublishinghouse@harvestways.org

ISBN 978-0-9567298-0-4

Cover photo © Paulo Images/Pulse Publishing House U.K

Cover design and typesetting by Wordzworth Limited, London, England

Printed in England by *Lightning Source UK Ltd.*

Contents

Preface

Sages of different times have reasonably come to the same conclusion: history always tends to repeat itself. This book contains practical, *easy-to-do* guides on how you will not repeat the costly mistakes made by others faced with a fresh opportunity to begin anew after suffering a heavy setback.

With more than a hint in different places of the prophetic anointing endued me, I have been prompted by God's Holy Spirit to highlight in a reader-friendly way how you can profit through life's crises.

Jealously guard and secure that which God has ordained for you as you put into practice these words of wisdom.

Happy reading.

Sammy Joseph

Birmingham
United Kingdom
October, 2010.

Chapter 1

A Takeover Bid

As *powers* change hands and spiritual transfer of blessings foretold by the Lord in His Word become manifested in the lives of the saints, I have been inspired by God's Holy Spirit to sound you a note of caution. A caution that would require you to "look before you leap!"

In 2 Samuel 20:1-10, we read of an interesting account of a takeover plot that was hatched by the very closest people to King David – aimed at de-throning him from the throne of Israel, an everlasting seat covenanted to the king and the tribe of Judah by God!

My hope is that this story will provide essential checklists to anyone willing to *step into shoes* ordained of God for them as well as checkmating the mutineers!

Let us read:

> *"And there happened to be there a man of Belial, whose name was Sheba, the son of Bichri, a Benjamite: and he blew a trumpet, and said, We have no part in David, neither have we inheritance in the son of Jesse: every man to his tents, O Israel.*

So every man of Israel went up from after David, and followed Sheba the son of Bichri: but the men of Judah clave unto their king, from Jordan even unto Jerusalem.

And David came to his house at Jerusalem; and the king took the ten women his concubines, whom he had left to keep the house, and put them in ward, and fed them, but went not in unto them. So they were shut up unto the day of their death, living in widowhood.

Then said the king to Amasa, Assemble me the men of Judah within three days, and be thou here present.

So Amasa went to assemble the men of Judah: but he tarried longer than the set time that he had appointed him.

And David said to Abishai, Now shall Sheba the son of Bichri do us more harm than did Absalom: take thou thy lord's servants, and pursue after him, lest he get him fenced cities, and escape us.

And there went out after him Joab's men, and the Cherethithes, and the Pelethites, and all the mighty men: and they went out of Jerusalem, to pursue after Sheba the son of Bichri.

When they were at the great stone which is in Gibeon, Amasa went before them. And Joab's garment that he had put on was girded unto him, and upon it a girdle with a sword fastened upon his loins in the sheath thereof; and as he went forth, it fell out.

And Joab said to Amasa, Art thou in health, my brother?

And Joab took Amasa by the beard with the right hand to kiss him.

But Amasa took no heed to the sword that was in Joab's hands: so he smote him therewith in the fifth rib, and shed out his bowels to the ground, and struck him not again; and he died! So Joab and Abishai his brother pursued after Sheba the son of Bichri.

(2 Samuel 20:1-10)

A closer look at David

On the one hand, King David's life story affords us a snap-shot view of him as a very versatile instrumentalist, successful songwriter, an anointed and a triumphant military commander with a strong messianic connection!

On the other hand, David – like you and I – was a mere human. The frailties in his fabric revealed a man who struggled with the lust of the flesh, lacked strong parental authority over his children and sometimes, was an hesitant king overwhelmed by emotions too strong for him to make a reasonable decision on his own. (I have shed more light on David's weaknesses in Chapter 3 of the book).

A Word on Joab

Joab, David's military second-in-command knew the king and could *read* him like a book. Afterall, he was a close relative. A nephew of David's – and of course, one of the original four-hundred disgruntled, depressed and indebted line-up starter recruits that formed David's army, Joab, now well trained and invested upon by the skilled king had ascended the ranks through the years, to become David's most senior general!

However, Joab was becoming too big for his own shoes! He began to scheme and plot against the king. The relationship between himself and his king gradually deteriorated from being celebrated to being simply tolerated. Joab had eventually progressed down a spiral loop!

King David's life story affords us a snap-shot view of him as a very successful singer. The other side of the coin depicted him as a man who struggled with the lust of the flesh, a weak father – and as, sometimes an hesitant king, overwhelmed by emotions too strong for him to make a reasonable decision on his own.

The cause of the downward spin?

David himself: His brazen, uncouth act with Bathsheba and its consequences. *Here is a key lesson for all in leadership: jealously guard the respect of those whom they lead by leading a transparent lifestyle of integrity and purity.* Self-respect genders respect of self.

Joab had lost all respect for David when he had received Uriah's execution letter that had been sealed with the king's seal! That seemed a while ago, but the memories that had led to that dastardly act by the king would never leave Joab. He began to detest and resist the king from his heart, thus paving the way for rebellion. Inner rebellion – much like inner peace – has a way of manifesting to the outside for all to see. That day of *manifestation* of Joab's demon wasn't too far off!

Soon enough, in a day of peace, at the transition from Saul's reign to David's when Abner, Saul's army general came to make peace with David, Joab would murder Abner cold blooded, in vengeance of the death of his brother Asahel. [1]

Years later, Joab dilly-dallied round Absalom, David's son who engaged in a mutinous revolt and a bloody attempt to overthrow his father in order to inherit the throne of Israel. This was an opportunity Joab deemed too good to be missed to potentially hurt the king. In a calculated quick move, he switched his allegiance and loyalty from David to Absalom. This indeed, was David's mid-life crisis hour!

Could you recall of any whom you (or another) have trained and invested upon time and effort over the years suddenly decamp for either your friend's, a close relative's – or an outright enemy's in a fierce battle to overthrow you? Are you currently going through a battle of *self-identity* or *self-discovery* which a friend-turned-to-fiend is scheming to capitalize upon? You surely will identify with this strategic junction in beloved King David's life!

Who becomes your trust during life's crisis could prove determinant in the actualization of your destiny!

PRAYER

Please pray this prayer aloud:

> *"Lord, You are the Friend that sticks closer than a brother. You were betrayed by your very closest friend while on earth. You know the potential instability of a soul in moments filled with the turbulence of life's crises. You overcame and became triumphant over all disappointments. You eventually rose again, becoming the LORD of all!*
>
> *Cause me today to be freshened up by Your precious Holy Spirit. Let His gentleness guide and lead me. Give me the courage to listen to Your guidance in the dark moments of my life.*
>
> *In Jesus' name. Amen."*

Chapter 2

Trust, A Question of Choice

I f you have had a trusted friend or close family relative like Joab turn against you in betrayal, this seems logical the exact question to ask: "Can I ever trust again?"

Now, to either trust or not trust after a disappointment is an inevitable conscious choice we must all make. I cannot de-emphasize the significant damage caused by the *paralysis* we allow to be injected into our veins, when because of a past hurt, we close up and become resigned to new ventures of life. True, a new stranger may not look very much different to the old acquaintance, but would you please take to heart that we are admonished never to stop entertaining strangers because we may, unknown to us be in the presence of the *very* angel sent for our rescue? [1]

"How then can I begin to trust again, after a hurt?" you seem to ask! Your question-type usually is fielded by those whose trust in, dependence on or loyalty to another has been grossly abused. You may have been jilted in a relationship – that started out promising – and in which you have heavily invested time, efforts and capital. (But I always say that it is better to have a broken investment than a mangled destiny. The shame, disappointment and heartbreak resulting from a broken engagement, for instance, are far much easier to handle than those that may result from a broken marriage).

You may have been divorced and left to pick the shattered pieces: the divorce being forced upon you because your spouse maligned, violated, or despised the marriage covenant. Your particular situation may be a business partner tricked you into signing beneath the dotted line, then botched and stitched you up in a financial stunt. Your emotions and personality are just awakening from such an outlandish rude violation and breach of trust – then, a while later; an opportunity to start all over again presents itself!

How do you navigate this season of *your* life while ensuring you do *not* shut the potential graceful door the Lord may be availing unto you?

Approaching Fresh Opportunities after a Crisis

Let me offer you five suggestions on how to approach new, fresh opportunities that present themselves after a crisis.

1.   Start with forgiveness that leads to healing and restoration.

Offended people *need* to ask God for His forgiveness for the part they played contributing to that last heart-wrenching disappointment they experienced. For example, engaging in the *sin of avoidance or omission* can lead to catastrophic avalanches in relationships: friendships, marriages, business partnerships and family accords.

Some situations could have been saved by advice or counseling. Some behavioral patterns that had demanded 'tough love' being administered so that restoration of the offensive person could have been readily brought to light and nipped in the bud had been tolerated or avoided. The offensive party deemed they were in the right and their *way of life* was understood and thus acceptable, when infact they had been tolerated and condoned. So they progressed in their iniquity. And the end result? Your disappointment! Your permissiveness in this case would have been your contributory part that led to *their* destruction – and *your* damage.

The goodnews is that our God is a God mercy. In His will, He allows mercy to rejoice against judgment. He restores the years the locust and cankerworm ate. He does give beauty for ashes – and He's interested in your wholesomeness.

Therefore, if you were involved in a crisis with another person for instance, there are three levels of relational well being from which you are expected to seek and pursue forgiveness, healing and restoration vis-à-vis: God; the offensive/offended (other) party; and yourself.

Be bold to ask God for His forgiveness. *"He will not always chide: neither will he keep his anger for ever."* (Ps. 103:9)

Then, if humanly possible without exposing yourself to any risks, ask for the forgiveness of the other party. You do not need to see them face to face. A call may do – if they will answer it. If they do not answer, leave them a straight-to-the-point message to let them know your intent. Or you may write them a succinct letter of apology or an email. Whether they forgive – and genuinely release you or not should not be your prerogative, but you have played a rightful part now.

Also, learn to forgive yourself!

As you start exfoliating the toxic layers of unforgiveness and exhuming the possible network roots of bitterness underlaid over time, you ask God to heal the past unpleasant experience that brought about the hurt – and bind up your wound. God will hear that prayer to heal and bind up, though healing time really depends on *you!*

2.   *Allow time element for your healing.*

Time heals. So be patient. We are admonished to *"let endurance and steadfastness and patience have full play and do a thorough work."* [2] In other words, take a break. Book a holiday. Leave the scene of the mishap if possible and desire time to be with yourself and no one else. This time spent alone should be invested as a time of reflection. Take time to reflect on what you should have done which you hadn't done. Let it be a time of you, mourning your loss. Grief is healthy and restorative – if done *not* in an overtone.

Do not enter the *re-bound game* at this time if you were just out of a failed relationship. Do not enter another business alliance so quickly. Take time to let the fogs clear off – and they certainly will.

3.   *Make 'guided' efforts; set godly, healthy boundaries.*

Faith and works must go hand in hand as Apostle James wrote in his letter. [3] All prayer and no action leads to futility just as all action and no prayer yields frustrations. Therefore, not only must you pray, but you also must make cognitive efforts at ensuring restoration. You must perceive and learn to 'open the door' again this time, more carefully; not all at once, but gradually!

How do you achieve this cognitive, evolving, self-learning? You do this employing what I refer to as *Noah's Cognitive Strategy*. Noah adopted a workable method to determine the suitability of earth's sustenance of life again at the abatement of the waters after the Great Flood. This is depicted in the eighth chapter of the book of Genesis.

At first, Noah sent a raven, a bird of prey. He then studied the raven's transitory migratory pattern as going forth and back from the ship, scavenging. After sometime, he sent a dove (the symbol of peace) – a home-bound bird specie – unlike the predatory and migratory raven. He watched and recorded the dove's pattern until someday the *bird of peace* returned with a newly sprouted, freshly plucked olive leaf in her bill, suggesting the existence of life on the new earth.

Seven days later – a number which symbolizes God's completion and rest – Noah sent again the same dove. He waited as usual until the evening, but this time, the dove had found her rest. In total, Noah's perceptive learning took about two hundred and fifty-six days; but at the end, he got the results he wanted.

You too can first send your *raven*. Someday, I am certain you will be able to send your *dove*. And when *your* dove finds her rest, you too would have found your footing! In other words, open the doors gradually and carefully. Like Noah, test the grounds. Wait a while, studying for signs of scavenging or predator-like features in the new openings you are presented with. Wait again, and be patient until your *peace symbol* returns to you bearing an olive leaf – its complimentary peace symbol – in its bill.

Set godly, realistic, achievable boundaries as checkmarks. Yes, *boundaries!* This is the word we have come to dislike because of its connection to the required discipline of the body, mind and spirit.

> *This is how boundary-setting works: if the new person coming into your life or the new opportunity availed unto you will not honor the healthy boundaries you have set; they may just not be your right shoe size.*

But in order not to fall short, yet once again; godly, healthy boundaries must be set! And this is how boundary-setting works: if the new person coming into your life or the new opportunity availed unto you will not honor the healthy boundaries you have set; they may just not be your right *shoe size*. They may be oversized or just too tight! In either case, you wouldn't want to slip your feet into such *opportunities* that may later hurt, causing you blisters and corns.

Take for instance a nursing sister who works hectic hours and gets only a day or two off duty in between weeks. She has specifically made her timetable of availability known to her intending friend with a clear warning: "Please do not call me at work hours. You may leave me a message onto my home telephone number." Despite their time together daily, on her way from work, her boyfriend decides to ignore her request – and in the name of love, calls her incessantly at midnight at work, not once, twice nor thrice, but all week long.

You must realize that such a caller isn't demonstrating love at all, neither does he possess an understanding of what *love* entails. He may rightly have possessive love or he could be a potential stalker with horrible pictures in his little mind. On another hand, he may be hunted by fear – incomplete love – pertaining to the *rendezvous* stories he had heard growing up as a little boy, of what had occasionally transpired between nurses and doctors! Whatever the case, such a guy has got *issues*. Advisably, such a man *may* not be well matched to the nursing sister as a marriageable mate. She may need to lovingly confront him and get them both talking and praying over matters; the sooner she acknowledged her predicament and initiated action, the better!

4. *Employ the services of trusted watchmen.*

In ancient kingdoms, cities were fortified with walls built to shut intruders out. On top of these walls were watchmen helping to guard the lives and the wellbeing of the city-dwellers from attackers – particularly through the *watches of the night.*

In biblical Israel, there were four *watches* of the night; these were times when people either were retiring from a hard day's labor, or rested in at night. At such times, *watchmen* were required to be awake and vigilant of suspicious moves.

In the same vein, it is wise to make yourself accountable to some spirit-led trusted friends who have their heads leveled on their shoulders to help you mount up spiritual watchfulness against potential *birds of prey*. These friends will watch over your boundaries too, in prayers and all spiritual *"watchings."*

5.   *Boost your confidence level.*

Even though it may not sound so spiritual, yet if you've got some fleece, like Gideon, then by all means *put 'em fleece out* as you test the ground. This act should be a confidence booster for you having being demoralized in the past.

You cannot afford to loose your self-confidence now; rather you've got to engage both hands on deck and do all it requires to boost your morale. The Scripture says *"Cast not away your confidence which has a great recompense of reward."* [4]

PRAYER

Would you want to please kindly pray this prayer aloud?

> *"Father LORD, help me to be able to freely and unconditionally forgive ALL who have wronged me – just as you have forgiven me.*
>
> *Give me the strength to mount up with the wings of the Eagle. Heal and restore me – in every way.*
>
> *Restore unto me the years that the waster had taken from me even as Your word promised in Joel 2:18.*
>
> *Renew me again by your Spirit.*
>
> *In Jesus' name. Amen."*

Chapter 3

Stability in Crisis

I t sure does sound like an oxymoron: "Stability in Crisis", yet a major difference between winners and losers is how they choose to manage the crises they undergo.

There are lessons to be learned in the aftermath of every crisis just as much as there are profits to be made. Winners over life's issues surely are better crises managers than losers because they have malleable hearts. Such were described by prophet Jeremiah as having *"an heart of flesh."* [1] Winning hearts are teachable, nimble hearts often able to spot the hidden opportunities inherent in each challenge they are faced with. Undoubtedly, Prophet Micah heard God rightly about gaining *light* in crises that he wrote: *"Rejoice not against me, O my enemy! When I fall, I shall arise; when I sit in darkness, the Lord shall be a light unto me."* [2]

The Certainty of Crisis in Life

There are more than enough scriptures in the Bible that lay to rest your doubts whether or not you will experience some turbulence in your life's flight. I will refer to two references such as:

> *"When thou passest through the waters, I will be with thee; and through the rivers, they shall not overflow thee: when thou*

walkest through the fire, thou shalt not be burned; neither shall the flame kindle upon thee."

(Isaiah 43:2)

Now, what would any rational being be doing waddling in deep, un-passable rivers except the currents are becoming overwhelming? What excitement is there walking through *the* fire other than to be burned?

> *There are more than enough scriptures in the Bible that lays to rest your doubts whether or not you will experience some turbulence in your life's flight.*

You may currently have been hauled into the furnace of rejection particularly by those who are meant to be the closest: family and friends. It seems as if you're alone as you struggle with the high tides of life. Listen to the psalmist:

"When my father and mother forsake me, then the LORD will take me up."

(Ps. 27:10)

Notice both Prophet Isaiah's and the Psalmist's use of the word of certainty "When." Then, it is of a certainty that we will experience some hardships, troubles or crises in life.

More comforting, however, is the understanding we are afforded by the Word of God that our Heavenly Father will be there with us in the middle of our troubles to deliver us. Most gloriously, we are assured that God will through those troubles fashion out for us, escape routes, if we remain steadfast in love with and worship of Him. [3] Jesus intimates us:

"In the world ye shall have tribulation: but be of good cheer; I have overcome the world."

(John 16:33b)

What a comforting assurance!

If you are undergoing any trouble whatever, rest assured by the Holy Spirit that your trouble will of itself be transformed into a stepping stone of glory!

Necessarily though, I have discovered – and would love to share with you – at least four basic, *must-have* attitudes that will ensure both your stability and profiting in *any* crisis of life.

Four Attitudes That Will Earn You Dividends in Crisis

1.   Ensure you secure God's presence.

A Jewish fable was once told of a mother shark and her little pups that went on a maiden deep-water expedition, and a predator fish that had for so long, swung the reign of terror over other territorial fishes in the water. One of the little sharks had suddenly been disoriented by the turbulent waves – and had lost its navigational bearings. Yet, this terror-king predator dared not instigate an attack against the helpless pup! Asked later by his peers why he couldn't prey on the straying little shark, he replied that he could see – not too far away, throughout the course of the little rebel's pleasurable *stroll* – the shadow of Mother Shark, luring!

David said: *"Yes, though I walk through the [deep, sunless] valley of the shadow of death, I will fear or dread no evil."* (Psalms 23:4; AMP.) How could David not fear or dread any evil in the deep, sunless, dark-pitched valley of the shadow of death? The answer is found in his awareness of God's all protective presence: *"For You are with me"*, he wrote!

Every good teacher knows the importance of establishing *a presence* in the classroom early enough in the new term: it settles once and for all the notion of *who* the boss is in that space. In the same vein, divine presence enforces absolute control over every threat of disruption from the devil and his cohorts. Securing divine presence is like dwelling in the *eye of the storm!*

Remember the three Hebrew men hauled into the fiery furnace? The Son of God himself had descended into the furnace to comfort them, and they had not been scorched! They had come out radiant – and so will you, if you will just secure Father God's presence amid your storms. But beware: sins like unforgiveness, bitterness, anger, wrath, pride, and lusts of any kind – to mention a few – must all be far removed from you because they will stay God's mighty presence away. Cohabiting with sin of any kind makes you become susceptible to predator attacks!

2.   Ensure an unwavering trust and sole dependence on His Word.

Not only must you ensure that you constantly secure God's presence, you must anchor your soul on His Word. Envision a ship in the midst of a fierce tempest. The most basic, primary safety operation the crew performs – before lightening the ship – is to let down the anchor(s).

We too have an anchor for our souls against tempestuous days in the Word of God! Like the captain and the crew of the troubled ship, we must lower *the anchor*. We must get serious with our daily study of and meditation upon the Word. This is the secret place David advised us to dwell at:

> *"He who dwells in the secret place of the Most High shall remain stable and fixed under the shadow of the Almighty [Whose power no foe can withstand]."*

(Ps. 91:1; AMP.)

3.   Do not loose your self worth.

God is present with you in trouble. More, His Word is your resting place. Now, you must take inventory of – and engage your total self-worth.

What is a person's self-worth?

Jesus confirms: *"A man's life consisteth not in the abundance of things which he possesseth."* [4] In other words, a person's self-worth is unquantifiable; it is of an inestimable price! *Having or not having money, a fleet of cars, houses and lands, fame, affluence, children – and so on, cannot compare with a person's true self-worth.*

What then is your *self-worth?* It is the sum total of how you perceive of yourself on the inside, which you subconsciously and inevitably portray to others. For instance, if you have a wrong, under-estimated self-perception of yourself, the strong chances are that you will end up having a low self-esteem. Someone else may have a false over-estimation of themselves and thus be proud, critical, despiteful, hateful and looking down on others less privileged than they.

Discovering and Affirming Your Self-worth

Crises times are not time to *dis-engag*e from self evaluation; rather, they provide us with ample opportunities for *inward-looking*. A crisis could reveal the deposit the Creator placed within us before the earth's foundation – if we are bold and smart enough to press into that discovery and affirm *us*. Relevant to our discussion, I believe, is the Walt Disney story.

Soon after his return from France where he had served as a chauffeur driving Red Cross officials during World War I, Walt Disney started a company called *Laugh-O-Grams* which eventually fell bankrupt. With his suitcase packed and lesser than $50, he headed for Hollywood for a fresh start.

By December 21, 1937, *Snow White and the Seven Dwarfs* – the first full-length animated musical feature – premiered at a theater in Los Angeles. The film produced was at a whopping cost of $1.5million US dollars – and that at the very heart of the Great Depression.

You too may require a new start. But you equally will need to discover and affirm your self-worth, first!

How do you *discover* your self worth?

Again, let us consider Walt. At age 7, on the farmlands of Marceline, Missouri where he was raised, young Disney developed interest in painting – and had sold his *work* to neighbors! The real discovery of his self worth occurred at age 17 while he was driving the ambulance in France during the War. His ambulance had been covered from stem to stern, not with stock camouflage, but with Disney cartoons. *Hence, a person discovers their self worth when they willingly reach inward so as to produce or give a thing – or indeed, render a service in the face of either danger or opportunity, yet without awaiting or demanding a pay in return.*

And how do you *affirm* your self-worth?

While self-worth discovery entails looking *inward*, self affirmation requires pressing *outward*; that is, applying pressure to your inner discovery. This, more than often times, employs the services of regimented self motivation and self discipline!

A guy who was laid off work surely *can* discover his self worth in the face of danger or opportunity staring him in the face. He *will* likely affirm his self worth thus: set his alarm clock to an early rising time, say 5.30 a.m. or 6 a.m. – whichever is agreeable to, by him and the Holy Spirit. He proceeds to give thanks to the Father for the gift of a brand new day. He searches the scriptures that line up with seeking a gainful employment or that relate to the wisdom of God in creating the *seen* world from the *unseen*. He verbalizes those key – one or two – scripture verses, making sure his mouth and heart align in perfect symphony with what God said in His words. Then, he dresses up nicely; checking himself in the mirror as he outwardly confesses before leaving his abode:

> *"Father, thank you for this great soul the company laid off. Thanks for the wisdom of God that is profitable to direct.*
>
> *Now, I go searching for that promotion You have disguised for me to find; I discover and receive it this day because of the favor of God that is upon my life. In Jesus' name."*

For another, it may be God intended for you to start a business or establish your *very* company, recession notwithstanding! (Remember Disney's $1.5 million production cost of the *Snow White and the Seven Dwarfs* in deep recession in America?) You must have faith in *you*!

Lacking confidence, feeling lethargic, and allowing the spirit of heaviness and depression to settle way down on the inside of you will lead to despondency that breeds failure. Rather, you must evaluate your self-worth, pull yourself together and *press* onward toward *"the mark"* which you have been called. [5]

4. *Tell yourself, "I am worth more than this!"*

You may be the minister or the laity; the boss or the servant, but people have maligned you. They have talked about you behind your back to your detriment. Key family decisions that bear down on you serious consequences were possibly made by unscrupulous family members who disregarded your consent being sought – and quite characteristically so, in your absence! Any of these situations is enough to make you feel worthless.

Probably your *ex* did *the dirty* on you. They ditched you and ran away with a younger blood. Now, you despise yourself? Oh, probably their misdemeanor is inducing you to want to *run around* for a little bit, too?

Common, pull your emotions together. Stop thinking silly. Stop meditating unwholesome thoughts; you're *worth more than this!*

Given, in retrospect, in any of these circumstances mentioned, there are some things you would have chosen to do or say differently, if you *had* the chance. But that is exactly what you now *have*: the chance and the opportunity to start afresh – and wisely!

Be grateful to God that you are equipped for the next *shoes* He's ordained just for you. Confess aloud to yourself: *I am fearfully and wonderfully made. I am amiable. I have the favor of the Almighty God on my life. People will like me, honor me and fall for my virtues.*

More, the Bible exhorts the believer to declare with their mouths, their redemption: *"Let the redeemed of the Lord say so ..."* [6] Guess what? You *say* so! Say it aloud, like you mean it: *I am mightily blessed and not cursed. No weapon formed against me shall prosper, and every wayward tongue that speaks ill about me, I condemn. I am the seed of Abraham: I am equipped to be the best.*

For you embroiled in a legal battle, *say*: *I emerge 'head' always. I am the head and not the tail. I win easy. I triumph because my Advocate, Jesus Christ, has blotted out and removed out of the way all handwriting of legalities that are against me. God is my Vindicator; I will be vindicated. I will be recompensed all my losses, in Jesus' name.*

Have you been waiting for a godly spouse? Declare your redemption thus: *I am beautiful, in and out. I am godly; hence I attract the godly one meant for me. God is ordering my steps unto that godly spouse. They'll find me, and I, them! We shall not mistake each other for another person's. I shall not lack my mate.*

Hold your head high with respect and dignity. Wait and prepare yourself in faith and with high expectations for *the* new opportunities Heaven is bringing your way. Pursue your daily life with a purpose – even with an assurance of the fact that *you are worth more than you suffered or lost!* Never let go of your confidence. Life couldn't get better with you realizing and affirming the *stuff* you're made of!

> *"And do not [for a moment] be frightened or intimidated in anything by your opponents and adversaries, for such [constancy and fearlessness] will be a clear sign (proof and seal) to them of [their impending] destruction, but [a sure token and evidence] of your deliverance and salvation, and that from God."*
>
> (Philippians 1:28; AMP.)

David's Weaknesses

Notably, crises have a tendency of eroding our self worth! David's crises in life commenced shortly after he hewed down Goliath's head from off his shoulders: the incumbent King Saul called for his own head too in an outburst of rage fueled by deep insecurities and jealousy!

David fled for dear life. This was his first of flights of escape from death!

After some years had passed, and Saul had passed away, it pleased God to establish David on the throne He had promised him! Soon afterwards however, like a house attacked by subsidence, David began to gravitate towards his inner weaknesses. His first grievous offence – the *Bathsheba-gate* scandal would not go un-noticed by Heaven. His emotions would never again return to a healthy robust state by the time he began to reap the fruits of the seed he sowed in committing adultery with Bathsheba – and the eventual murder of Uriah, Bathsheba's husband. In due time, the baby conceived by the king through that unholy alliance would die despite David's prayers to God to spare his life.

The next string of events were catastrophic: his daughter Tamar was raped by her half brother, Amnon, David's eldest son. Amnon in turn, got killed by Absalom – the victim's brother and David's third son. Absalom would then hatch a thick mutinous plot: forcefully eject his father, David from the throne of Israel and plan to kill him, even while the king fled to exile, in the desert! The plan failed and Absalom was eventually killed by the incorrigible Joab! These were just personal losses to the king; let alone troop losses moderately estimated at 20 000 men, in this botched *coup d'état*.

How dark must the pitch of the night have been for David?

And though David – by the supernatural ordination of God – did ascend yet again the throne of Israel, the king had been pretty rattled by the sprouting of these unscheduled, unmitigated crises of his life, one after another!

You know, just like stitches burst at the seams due to applied pressure, so do our weaknesses begin to manifest when life's pressures are applied to the very core of our beings. The Bible never – in any of its records – did disguise the potential fallibility of mankind. Neither did David attempt to conceal his personal weaknesses. Thus, we are opportuned to catch a pristine glimpse of a weakened king unable to make ordinary common logical decisions. We also see a morally disillusioned father, lacking basic disciplinary procedures set in place for his errant sons – even when the law demanded it off him! [7]

And apart from *Bathsheba-gate*, the most pronounced of David's flaws was his inability to keep Joab in check!

Could it have been possible the king was so accustomed to Joab's indispensable military prowess and ingenuity that he couldn't dismiss him from service? Or he retained Joab in his cabinet out of loyalty to 'trademarks'?

Beware of Loyalty to expired *'trademarks'*

How many of us have held onto expired 'trademark' person or *landmarks* in our lives, to our own regrets?

Expired *trademark* people are the associates, the close family companions and friendly ties that have become ruptured beyond *all* construability!

> *Apart from Bathsheba-gate, the most pronounced of David's flaws was his inability to keep Joab in check!*

Do you hold onto a dead marriage where you are being abused, beaten, broken and decimated in the name of a fraternal or christian conscience? I beg to challenge you otherwise. I say that conscience of yours is a *"weak conscience"* [8] tending towards becoming *"seared"* [9] and *"defiled."* [10]

Now, the Bible makes us aware of the different types of conscience, three of which I have just mentioned; but the type of conscience God expects us to possess is that good and pure conscience, a *"conscience void of offence toward God and toward men."* [11] We are expressly commanded to nurture the spirit given us of God which is of *"love, power and a sound mind."* [12]

You can no longer afford to keep holding onto the *'trademark' feeling* of marital security depicted by the band-display on your fourth finger, when infact your spouse had repeatedly violated or cheated on you – not once, twice nor thrice. This has become their habit. They also had repeatedly assaulted you – in the presence of friends, families, and even, young growing children! To worsen matters, they kept avoiding counseling sessions booked and paid for by you!

Some of you are still holding onto the *family trademark* of attending a *dead* church, because your grandparents were among those who laid the foundations of that building a century ago, when you know it all too well that the Holy Spirit is challenging you to move on!

Lack of confidence, loyalty to expired *trademarks* and diminished self-worth are a monster. They rob of self confidence and power to effect necessary changes. They erode the *within*, the very core of a being – the actual place we are instructed to guard and fortify. [13]

> *Lack of confidence, loyalty to expired trademarks and diminished self-worth are a monster. They rob of self confidence. They erode the within, the very core of the being – the very place we are instructed to guard and fortify!*

The Holy Spirit, on the very day of Joab's copious rough speech and threats of abandonment to the king at hearing the unpleasant news of Absalom's death, had challenged David to replace the insulting war general in a cabinet re-shuffle that would have promoted Amasa and disinherited Joab. [14] David had dragged his feet and hadn't followed his conviction with a loud, official decision!

Truth be told: if we would continue to hold onto the 'old order', the expired ***'trademarks'*** *and the* **Joab's** *in our lives; why must we expect anything newer than depravity and mediocrity?*

Evidently, David had had enough of Joab's mischievousness since his murder of Abner, yet he lacked the required boldness and moral strength to get rid of him. [15] David's lack of self-belief cost the nation – including families and loved ones – the deaths of those thousands of soldiers at Absalom's treachery! [16] But wait. There will still be one or more bloody blunder caused by Joab! Or dare I say, David?

Joab's One More Costly Blunder

Amasa would be Joab's next bloody victim. Amasa had it coming since Absalom preferred him over Joab to lead his army against David at the revolt!

But my question still remains: *Why would King David still retain the services of Joab, Amasa or even Abishai to lead his reformed army?*

The answer is not far-fetched. It was because they were his close relatives. They were, unbeknown to him, the *expired trademarks* his weakened emotions still counted upon for emotional support in time of loneliness and need! But Amasa was struck down by Joab at an opportuned time!

The one upon whose arms you lean in the time of trouble has the capacity to re-launch or decimate your destiny. Be warned: *"Trust in the LORD for ever: for in the LORD JEHOVAH is everlasting strength."* (Isaiah 26:4)

PRAYER

Heavenly Lord, cause there to be heaven-sent destiny-helpers surround me in my hour of need. Let me always remember the wordings of the first stanza of the old hymn:

My soul is built on nothing less
Than Jesus' blood and righteousness
I dare not trust the sweetest frame
But wholly lean on Jesus' name

Refrain:
On Christ the solid Rock, I stand
All other ground is sinking sand
All other ground is sinking sand![17]

Chapter 4

Eight Essential Checklists to Consider Before Stepping Into Shoes

C ostly tragedies – like the death of Amasa – are preventable through the deployment of water-tight checklists.

    Earlier, at the beginning of this book, I explained the assurance that God has prepared for you who love Him, some divine 'takeovers' which will not at all require any manipulation, masterminding or scheming on your part to attain. There is *the* right pair of *shoe-size* you are about to divinely *slip on*; particularly after having suffered a tragedy or crisis. But there are also potential risks you run if you hold onto grief for too long or fail to securely learn to approach with trust, new doors of opportunities – and the new set of people He (God) is availing unto you. To further equip your mind, I shared with you the basic character trait which distinguishes winners from losers: their ability to crisis-manage, successfully!

Now, I am about to highlight – from the story in 2 Samuel 20:1-10 – eight essential checklists you must *not* fail to tick before *stepping into the shoes* that look seemingly assigned just for you! Here they are:

8 Essential Checklists

Checklist 1

Exercise caution when involved in matters involving contrasting family members' interests.

Joab and Abishai were David's nephews – as much as Amasa was! The *duo* however, were siblings – yet rival replacements for *the* top post in David's army. Do exercise restraints when involved in an embroiling circumstance involving blood relations.

Checklist 2

Exercise utmost caution when intending to overthrow the 'old order' in favor of the 'new order'; or in dealing with 'principalities' such as the Joab's of your life: they may be accursed or curse-procreating.

What did the biblical ancients do to accursed things? They offered them up in a physical fire as a "burnt sacrificial offering" unto the Lord, the Possessor of Heaven and earth.

But how can you offer a physical burnt offering in this modern era?

That should be very easy: it shouldn't take you long to find one or more blessed, fruitful, well anointed christian ministries or ministers of the gospel where you *plant* the accursed things as "burnt offerings" unto the Lord!

Now, whilst curses are spoken by words, accursed things need reside in your domain, be present in your field or be lodged in your bank accounts to activate *the* specific curse(s) for which they primarily required a residence.

So, to rid yourself of *the* curse(s) brought in by an accursed thing, person or property; you rid, or relieve yourself of those very things, people, and properties that have brought you an ill wind. Joshua got rid of the accursed things in the Israeli camp at Ai, starting with Achan! The captain and the crew lighted Jonah overboard the Spanish-bound ship before *their* sea calmed!

Obey the Word of God and verbalize God's blessings over you – and you will be free of curses engendered by the accursed. Do these and watch the Owner of all things revert unto you, untold blessings in the stead of the curses these "things" would have attracted unto you.

Checklist 3

Obtain and retain a legal proclamation of ascendancy unto authority, emancipation of power or clear demarcation of boundaries, rights and duties at all times.

Always obtain and retain original copies of legal documents particularly when dealing with circumstances, people or contracts that may want to resist or pose a challenge to ascertained progress ordained of God for your life. Amasa failed miserably at not obtaining a legal tender to serve Joab when he confronted him at the king's request. Little wonder *the* struggle with Joab ensued!

Checklist 4

When you begin to notice you are being confronted by the 'old order' and delayed beyond the reasonable time limit … call for help from the King.

Amasa tarried longer than the three-day-time limit the king had appointed him, yet he didn't deem it fit to inform David about his struggles *(verse 5)*.

On the other hand, arch-angel Gabriel, when confronted and held up – for twenty one days – in combat with the prince of Persia sent for Heaven's re-enforcements. Arch-angel Michael was quick on Heaven's dispatch. Otherwise, Daniel's requests could never have manifested in earthly realm. (Notice, "*the prince of Persia*" was the territorial demonic principality assigned to frustrate God's counsels over the named geographical region of Persia. He was not an earthly, physical prince!)

> *"Then said he unto me, Fear not, Daniel: for from the first day that thou didst set thine heart to understand, and to chasten thyself before thy God, thy words were heard, and I am come for thy words.*
>
> *But the prince of the kingdom of Persia withstood me one and twenty days: but, lo, Michael, one of the chief princes, came to help me: and I remained there with the kings of Persia."*
>
> (Daniel 10:12-13)

Because you fight not flesh and blood, but spiritual elements and entities, you must learn to radio the *Headquarter* for reinforcements. Be smart. Link up with others doing what you are doing. Pray with others who are of the same disposition as you! Do not tackle the *"principalities and powers"* alone; it may take you longer than twenty days (in delay) before you can break free. It may end up costing you more. Amasa fought alone. He died alone!

Checklist 5

Inquire about and dig out all you can about people and circumstances with whom you have dealing leaving no stone un-turned ... Offenders always have a pattern of carrying out offences that should serve as a clue and a warning to the wary.

Amasa should have known that Joab was a murderer who smote Saul's general Abner *"under the fifth rib"* (2 Sam. 3:27). That was a vital piece of knowledge he should have been armed with! You cannot afford to be so gullible, this second chance. You must arm yourself with every bit of information you can lay hold of about potential interests.

You have been offered to pay for a property, for instance. You would be "spot on" to make enquiries first, regarding the property. Delve into papers and documents lodged with the Council before making a bid! Do your research thoroughly. Google the names of anything – and I mean *everything*

– on the website. You will be amazed at how much information is at your finger tips, if you will dare to just lift those fingers!

Checklist 6

Be vigilant. Critically appraise and honestly evaluate – who/what's coming your way.

A lady has been praying for a godly man for spouse when she caught the semblance of a *quick* creature in trousers, dashing past her. Ensure you look carefully and ascertain that he's no chimp on the loose! (Same goes for the man believing God for a godly wife.) Some orangutans may have bolted out of their bounds on *God's day of rest*. You cannot afford to be caught napping. Be watchful, vigilant, prayerful and careful. Employ the use of *Noah's Cognitive Strategy*, if need be!

Amasa "*took no heed to the sword that was in Joab's hands*" *(verse 10)*.

He paid heavily for his non-vigilance.

Checklist 7

Deal with 'troubled people' from a distance …

There's an African saying which says: *"the calculated moves of a tiger on the prowl are not attributed to trepidation or lack of self belief; rather, to the contrary."*

Coupled with self confidence is this natural attribute inherent in us which we call *"first instincts."* Follow your first instincts; they have been put there by the Creator – as your protective mechanism – to flag off an imminent danger!

Deal with troubled people from a distance. This is how you recognize them: if someone, a project or a venture becomes an established victim of repeated misfortunes, it may be time to carry out a spiritual appraisal and inventory on them to consider their feasibility!

Amasa failed to distance himself from Joab's embrace. He lacked the "first instincts" to read in between the lines:

> *"And Joab said to Amasa, Art thou in health, my brother? And Joab took Amasa by the beard with the right hand to kiss him."*
>
> (Verse 9)

Checklist 8

Be objective and decisive about crucial decisions.

Any acquaintance, relative or confidant who de-camps from you in your mid-night hour is neither dependable nor reliable a person. Don't be caught in a web of sentimental feelings like David was. Swap your style of operations with unfaithful, mutinous friends and confidants:

> *A friend loves at all times, and is born, as is a brother, for adversity."*
>
> (Prov. 17:17; AMP.)

PRAYER

Please pray these words meditatively:

> *"Lord Jesus, please grant me the grace and the clarity of mind to always not compromise Your Word and expectations of me. You keep calling me higher.*
>
> *Help me, give the urge to forget those things which are behind and the surge to reach forth to those which are before me. Let me press, daily toward the mark of Your high calling for my life.*
>
> *In Jesus' name.*
>
> *Amen."*

Conclusion

My impression is that you will likely re-read this book, this time, with a ready pen and paper handy, checking off one after the other, these teachings the Holy Spirit has presented you so as to ensure the purity of the next pair of *shoes* you are about to step into.

If this message has impacted your decision-making in any way, please do kindly write me today to *reverendsammy@harvestways.org*

I am looking forward to hearing from you.

Should you love to invite Jesus in your heart as Savior and LORD – or re-dedicate your life to Him after seasons of disobedience and disloyalty to Him and His cause; kindly pray the following prayer with me:

> *"LORD Jesus Christ. I thank You that no matter what I have or haven't done, You always love me. I thank You for sacrificing Your life on the Cross, for me.*
>
> *This _____ day of the month _____ of 20 _ ; I repent of my sins. I ask You to come into my heart and live therein.*
>
> *I confess with my mouth that You are the LORD crucified, buried and raised up into glory – and the soon coming King. Come, from this day onward to reign in and rule my life by the Holy Spirit.*

Please write my name in the Lamb's Book of Life.

Thank you for doing this for me!

Amen."

Signed: _____

References

Chapter 1
[1.] *2 Samuel 3:12-39*

Chapter 2
[1.] *Hebrews 13:2*
[2.] *James 1:4, AMP.*
[3.] *James 2:14-20*
[4.] *Hebrews 10:35*

Chapter 3
[1.] *Ezekiel 36:26*
[2.] *Micah 7:8*
[3.] *Romans 8:28*
[4.] *Luke 12:15*
[5.] *Philippians 3:14*
[6.] *Psalms 107:2*
[7.] *Leviticus 18:9, 29*
[8.] *1 Corinthians 8:7*
[9.] *1 Timothy 4:2*
[10.] *Titus 1:15*
[11.] *Acts 24:16*
[12.] *2 Tim. 1:7*
[13.] *Proverbs 4:23*
[14.] *2 Samuel 19:5-7; 13*
[15.] *2 Samuel 3:28-29*
[16.] *2 Samuel 18:7*
[17.] *"My Hope is Built on Nothing Less", Edward Mote, 1797-1874. Copyrighted.*

Worship with Us

The Harvestways Int'l Church, (Birmingham, U.K.)

Holloway Community Hall,
Northfield, Birmingham
England, United Kingdom B31 1TT
Sundays: 12 noon- 2pm
Fridays: 7–8.30pm (House Fellowship)
Tel: (+44) 7906441276
(+44) 7854675159

The Harvestways Int'l Church (Nigeria, West Africa)

1 Harvest Way, Off Elewura Street
Behind Zartech / GLO Office,
Challenge G.P.O Box 2910
Dugbe, Ibadan Oyo State,
Nigeria, West Africa.
Sundays: 9am
Wednesdays: 6pm
Mobile: (+234) 8078198576
(+234) 8023928508

The Harvestways Int'l Church (South Africa)

20 Sipres Street
Eindhoven Delft South 7100
Capetown,
South Africa
Sundays: 9am – 11am
Wednesdays: 6pm
Mobile: (+27) 7436 55011
(+27) 732454884
(+27) 219555168

You may want to inquire about SJM, invite Rev. Sammy to minister for you or become a partner; please contact:

Sammy Joseph Ministries
P.O. Box 15129,
Birmingham,
West Midlands,
England
B45 5DJ
Mobile: (+44) 7906 441276
(+44) 7854 675159

Other Books by the Author

Other books by the author that can be ordered at all Christian book-shops near you, *Pulse Publishing House* or from our website *www.harvestways.org* include:

GIDEON: Releasing the Potentials Within You

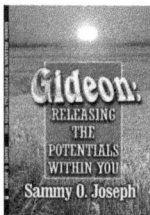

This book draws analogies from the life of Gideon (one of Israel's Judges) and applies them to how you can effectively release the hidden potentials within you. Written in easy, straightforward, simple language, you will find basic practical insights that will help lift you above common mediocrity levels in life! *(120 pages)*

DESTROYING THE POWER OF DELAY: Possessing Your Canaan

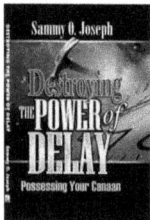

Best seller expository piece of writing. The author aims at showing you how to avoid the path that leads to a detour of destiny; 22 major causes of delay; how to maximally profit in delay and virtues that will enable you enter into and abide in your destiny. *(206 pages)*

Download *PULSE On-line*, freely at www.harvestways.org

You can purchase/order a copy of this book from Christian Bookshops across the nation.

Other outlets:

In the United Kingdom

The Harvestways Int'l Church
Holloway Hall, Ley Hill
Birmingham, England
B31 1TT

Sammy Joseph Ministries
Box 15129
Birmingham, England,
U.K
B45 5DJ
Tel: (+44) 7906441276
        (+44) 7854675159

In Africa

Pulse Publishing House
Plot 1, Harvest Way
Behind GLO Office
Old Challenge
G.P.O. Box 2910
Dugbe, Ibadan
Nigeria.
Mobile: (+234) 8136812070

Pulse Publishing House
351 Delft Main Road
Delft South, Capetown
South Africa
7100
Mobile: (+27) 7436 55011
         (+27) 732454884

On-line
@
www.amazon.co.uk, www.amazon.com, www.harvestways.org

www.ingramcontent.com/pod-product-compliance
Lightning Source LLC
Chambersburg PA
CBHW060949050426

42337CB00052B/3293